LEWIS UNIVERSITY

McDonald's:
What It Takes To Be A Leader

Deivis Ivanauskas
Kristina Stulgaite
Manzella Girolama

April 2012

This book has been written as part of the academic project in the Strategic Management class at Lewis University during the spring of 2012.

Table of Contents

I.	**Diagnosis**	**1**
	a. Mission	2
	b. Values	3
	c. Objectives	5
	d. Corporate Strategy	6
	e. Policies	7
	i. Diversity	7
	ii. Ethical Standards/Code of Conduct	8
	iii. Suppliers	10
	iv. Human Resources	12
	f. Strategic Managers and Board	13
	i. Senior Level Executives	14
	ii. Corporate Governance	15
	1. Responsibilities	16
	2. Board Committees	17
	3. Director Compensation	19
	iii. Generic Industry Type	20
	g. Organizational Structure	27
	h. Financial Analysis	29
	i. Graphs	29
	ii. Altman	50
	iii. Tobin's Q	51
	iv. DuPont Analysis	52
	i. SWOT Analysis	53
II.	**Focal Points For Action**	**55**
III.	**Development Alternatives**	**59**
	a. Generic Industry Type & Industry Characteristics	59
	b. Boston Consulting Group Matrix	60
	c. Rumelt's Criteria	63
	d. Competitive Position	65
	e. Competitive Strategy Options	66
IV.	**Decision and Recommendation**	**68**
	a. Corporate	68
	b. Business	68
	c. Functional	68
V.	**Implementation**	**69**
VI.	**Works Cited**	**71**

I. Diagnosis

McDonald's Corporation franchises and operates McDonald's restaurants in the global restaurant industry. These restaurants serve a varied, limited, value-priced menu in more than 100 countries around the world. All restaurants are operated either by it or by franchisees, including conventional franchisees under franchise arrangements, and foreign affiliated markets and developmental licensees under license agreements. The company and its franchisees purchase food, packaging, equipment and other goods from various independent suppliers. It offers a range of products. Independently owned and operated distribution centers, approved by it, distribute products and supplies to McDonald's restaurant's menu includes hamburgers and cheeseburgers, Big Mac, Quarter Pounder with Cheese, Fillet-O-Fish, several chicken sandwiches, Chicken McNuggets, Chicken Selects, Snack Wraps, French fries, salads, snakes, McFlurry desserts, sundaes, soft serve cones, pies and cookies.

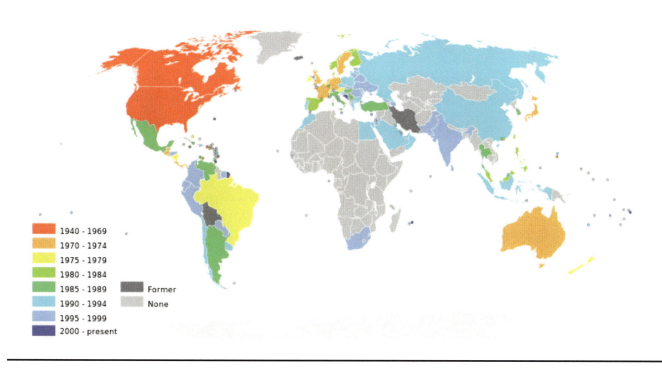

Figure 1: Countries with McDonald's Stores

Mission

McDonald's Corporation is determined to continuously improve their social and environmental performance. They work hard, together with their suppliers and independent restaurant franchisees, to strive toward a sustainable future – for the company and the communities in which we operate. From the beginning, they have been a company committed to doing the right thing. Today, their values continue to be the foundation for who they are, what they do, and how they operate.

McDonald's brand mission is to be their customers' favorite place and way to eat. Their worldwide operations are aligned around a global strategy called the Plan to Win, which center on an exceptional customer experience – People, Products, Place, Price and Promotion. They are committed to continuously improving their operations and enhancing their customers' experience.

Figure 2: McDonald's Logo

Values

MCDONALD's PRIORITIES: Achieving Sustainable Success

Figure 3: McDonald's Priorities: Achieving Sustainable Success

McDonald's places the customer experience at the core of all they do. Their customers are the reason for their existence. McDonald's Corporation demonstrates their appreciation by providing them with high quality food and superior service in a clean, welcoming environment, at a great value. Their goal is quality, service, cleanliness and value (QSC&V) for each and every customer, each and every time.

McDonald's Corporation is committed to their people. They provide opportunity, nurture talent, develop leaders and reward achievement. McDonald's believe that a team of well-trained individuals with diverse backgrounds and experiences, working together in an environment that fosters respect and drives high levels of engagement, is essential to our continued success.

They believe in the McDonald's System. McDonald's business model, depicted by their "three-legged stool" of owner/operators, suppliers, and company employees, is our foundation, and balancing the interests of all three groups is key.

McDonald's Corporation operates their business ethically. Sound ethics is good business. At McDonald's, they hold ourselves and conduct our business to high standards of fairness, honesty, and integrity. They are individually accountable and collectively responsible. McDonald's gives back to their communities. They take seriously the responsibilities that come with being a leader. We help our customers build better communities, support Ronald McDonald House Charities, and leverage our size, scope and resources to help make the world a better place.

McDonald's grows their business profitably. McDonald's is a publicly traded company. As such, we work to provide sustained profitable growth for our shareholders. This requires a continuous focus on their customers and the health of their system. McDonald's Corporation is continuously striving to improve. They are a learning organization that aims to anticipate and respond to changing customer, employee and system needs through constant evolution and innovation.

Objectives

The McDonald's Corporation strives to do the following as their objective:

- To serve good food in a friendly and fun environment.
- To be a socially responsible company.
- To provide good returns to its shareholders.
- To provide its customers with food of a high standard, quick service, and value for money.

Figure 4: Distribution of McDonald's Branches around the World

Corporate Strategy

McDonald's Corporation uses a single business unit strategy. In an effort to make the traditional business model less bureaucratic and more flexible, McDonald's Corporation has begun implementing single business unit strategy. Instead of forcing a new department into the standard chain of command, the corporation will form differently sized autonomous business units that report directly to top management. Now the role of the corporation is to manage its business units and coordinate their efforts into the overall corporate strategy.

A business unit is a section or department of a business that runs as an autonomous entity. Their profits are usually treated separately than those of the business as a whole. All SBUs (single business or collection of businesses), have their own competitors and a manager accountable for operations, and can be independently planned for.

Each business unit must meet five criteria. First, their mission and focus must be different from all other organization SBUs. Second, they should have an easily and clearly defined group of competitors. Third, it's planning and development should be carried out quite independently of any other business unity. Finally, each SBU must have a separate manager with decision-making authority who is fully responsible for the operation.

While there is no generic approach that works best all the time, once you determine an approach that works, it's best to stick with it. A collaborative approach builds business units by relying on employee input combined with corporate strategy. A corporate led approach relies on the executives to plan the unit and the goals focus on growth, profit and market share. Thirdly, the business unit may form its own strategic plan that is approved, edited or disapproved by corporate management.

Single business unit strategy relies on answering two questions: what are a unit's strengths and what is the best way to improve performance. This analysis allows you to establish the SBU's mission, setting objectives, and determining strategy to use to meet these objectives. SBUs require constant analysis through reports and financial projections to determine if they remain productive or if their strategy necessitates alteration to better improve performance.

Policies

McDonald's Corporation takes its policies to heart. One of the main policies which the corporation stands by is its inclusion and diversity. At McDonald's they are moving from awareness to action. Their goal is to have people within the organization working and living to reach their full potential. McDonald's believes that leaders hold themselves accountable for learning about, valuing, and respecting individuals on both sides of the counter. At McDonald's, diversity and inclusion is part of the culture – from the crew room to the Board Room. They are working to achieve this goal every day by creating an environment for everyone to contribute their best.

Quick Facts

70% women/minority US employees

over **25%** women/minorities in leadership

over **5 billion** diverse vendor spend

45% women/minority franchisees

Figure 5: Diversity Quick Facts

Ethical Standards/Code of Conduct

McDonald's believes in the business adage that the customer is important. They expect employees to be committed to their jobs and to their customers, and to behave as ambassadors of the company. They also believe that it is important to acknowledge the community that supports each McDonald's restaurant and to return that support to the community. A system was established to train each employee in more than just how to perform jobs technically. It requires a structured orientation that would teach the employee these ethical standards and more, as well as the attitude with which the job is to be performed.

Corporate social responsibility (CSR) or corporate citizenship entails companies behaving in a socially responsible manner, and dealing with other business parties who do the same. With growing public awareness and demand for socially responsible businesses, it is little wonder that companies of today take corporate social responsibility into account when planning future socially responsible business operations. Since the birth of McDonald's Corporation it has shown social responsibility achieving results and always maintaining open lines of communication with its customers and other key stakeholders.

One approach to engaging in corporate social responsibility is through community-based development projects. Community-based and community-driven development projects have become an important form of development assistance among global socially responsible companies. An economic relationship implies a strategy of engaging the wider community into the core business activity of the company so that communities become embedded in corporate supply chain strategy to create a sustainable business.

An example of this approach of McDonald's and its contribution to the communities is seen in launch of its Flagship Farms Initiative (FAI) in Europe. The program showcases seven progressive farms employing innovative farming practices across Europe and carries out research into how ethical farming practices can be incorporated into commercial farming systems. Another example is seen in the Sustainable Fisheries program which is in collaboration with the Sustainable Fisheries Partnership. This program defines sustainability standards that guide all of McDonalds's purchases worldwide for wild-caught fish that goes into making those Fillet-o-Fish and make the relevant fishery a more sustainable business.

McDonald's also donates a portion of its pre-tax profits to corporate philanthropy as part of its efforts to be more socially responsible. McDonald's makes charitable contributions through the Ronald McDonald House Charities (RMHC) which aims to create, find and support programs that directly improve the health and well-being of children.

According to Clara Carrier of Ronald McDonald House Charities, in particular, the Ronald McDonald Care Mobile attempts to ensure that children in vulnerable communities can receive state-of-the-art medical and dental treatment to improve their health and strengthen the whole family. This health care on wheels program attempts to change children's lives and improve communities along the way.

Figure 6: Ronald McDonald House Charities Logo

Suppliers

The McDonald's supply chain is a complex web of direct and indirect suppliers. They manage this complex system by working with direct suppliers who share their values and vision for sustainable supply. McDonald's hold them to clear standards for quality, safety, efficiency and sustainability. The McDonald's Corporation expects to extend these requirements to their suppliers. They also partner with them to identify, understand and address industry-wide sustainability challenges and achieve continuous improvement. Overall, McDonald's and their suppliers are collectively focused on three areas of responsibility: ethics, environment, and economics.

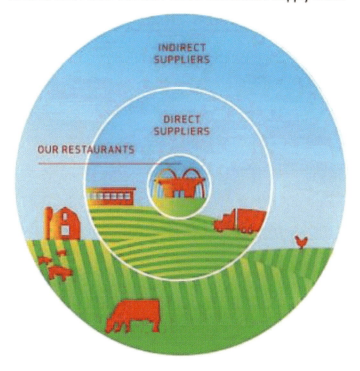

Figure 7: Supply Chain

McDonald's Corporation envision a supply chain that profitably yields high-quality, safe products without supply interruption while leveraging their leadership position to create a net benefit by improving ethical, environmental and economic outcomes. They envision purchasing from suppliers that follow practices that ensure the health and safety of their employees and the welfare and humane treatment of animals in our supply chain. McDonald's envision influencing the sourcing of our materials and ensuring the design of our products, their manufacture, distribution and use to minimize life-cycle impacts on the environment. Lastly they envision delivering affordable food, engaging in equitable trade practices, limiting the spread of agricultural diseases, and positively impacting the communities where our suppliers operate.

Human Resources

Although some level of consent is always necessary, control is high on the agenda at McDonald's. Control at McDonald's is not merely achieved by direct supervision, machines, the physical layout of the restaurant and the detailed prescription of rules and procedures but also through recruitment. Even unskilled workers have some power to disrupt the efficiency of the operation by withdrawing co-operation from the production process, disrupting the process or by simply leaving the organization. Employees may submit to the authority of the employer, but are always likely to retain a strong interest in the use of their labor. Employees and management are, therefore, to some extent *interdependent*; management cannot rely solely on coercion or even compliance to secure high performance, management also needs to secure active employee consent and co-operation.

Identification with the restaurant and other crew members is fostered through the creation of a new form of collective. If 'us and them' is still recognized, it is reinterpreted to mean 'us' as the management and crew and 'them' as the customer. Workers are encouraged to think of themselves as part of a team and managers are encouraged to equate restaurant management with coaching a team. The result of this form of teamwork seems to be that individuals are often loath to be seen by their peers as making extra work for other people by not doing their share. Even the more resentful employees, who had what management saw as negative attitudes, would still work hard to keep the respect of their peers. A typical feature of management style was the repeated use of certain kinds of language, with paternalistic expressions such as the McDonald's family. Management and employees in both countries used the term to describe their work environment. Many responses reflected the strongly paternalistic nature of the employment relationship which management worked to foster.

Strategic Managers and Board

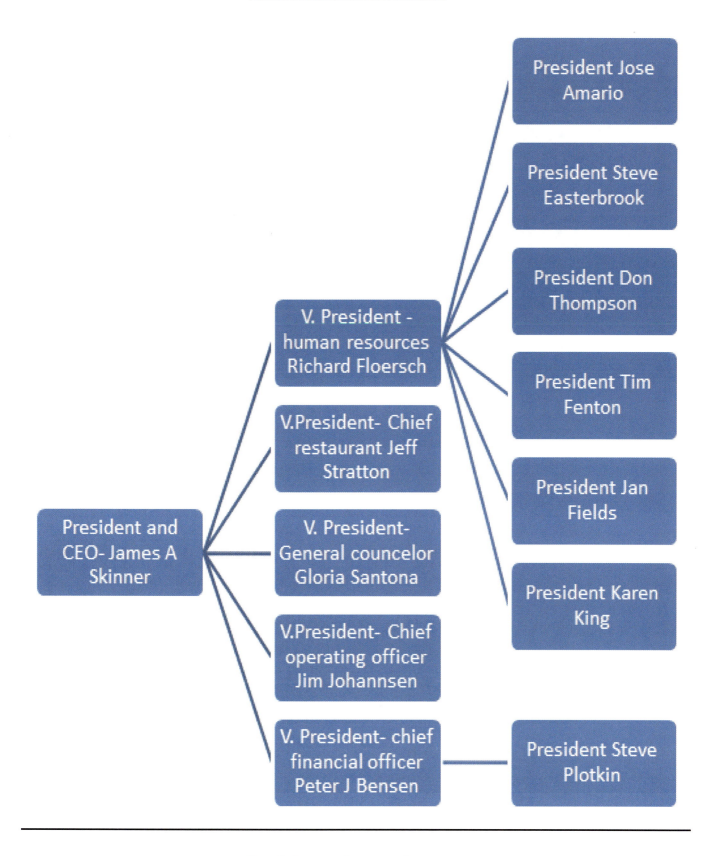

Figure 8: Corporate Governance Structure

Senior Level Executives

Leadership

Jim Skinner - CEO
Vice Chairman and Chief Executive Officer

Don Thompson
President and Chief Operating Officer

Mike Andres
Central Division President, McDonald's USA

Jose Armario
Corporate Executive Vice President Worldwide Supply Chain, Development, & Franchising

Peter J. Bensen
Executive Vice President and Chief Financial Officer

Tim Fenton
President of Asia, Pacific, Middle East and Africa

Jan Fields
President, McDonald's USA, LLC

Richard Floersch
Executive Vice President - Chief Human Resources Officer

Doug Goare
President, McDonald's Europe

Jim Johannesen
Executive Vice President, Chief Operations Officer, McDonald's USA

Karen King
East Division President - McDonald's USA

Kevin Newell
Chief Brand Officer

Steve Plotkin
West Division President - McDonald's USA

Gloria Santona
Executive Vice President, General Counsel and Secretary

Jeff Stratton
Executive Vice President and Worldwide Chief Restaurant Officer

Fred L. Turner
Honorary Chairman

Figure 9: McDonald's Corporation Leadership

Corporate Governance

"The basis for our entire business is that we are ethical, truthful and dependable. It takes time to build a reputation. We are not promoters. We are business people with a solid, permanent, constructive ethical program that will be in style years from now even more than it is today." - Ray Kroc, 1958

McDonald's success is built on a foundation of personal and professional integrity. Hundreds of millions of people around the world trust McDonald's. McDonald's Corporation earns that trust everyday by serving safe food, respecting their customers and employees and delivering outstanding Quality, Service, Cleanliness and Value (QSC&V). McDonald's Corporation builds on this trust by being ethical, truthful and dependable. In short, what Ray Kroc, founder of McDonald's Corporation said more than 50 years ago was right!

Responsibility

McDonald's Board of Directors is entrusted with and responsible for the oversight of McDonald's Corporation in an honest, fair, diligent and ethical manner. The Board has long believed that good corporate governance is critical to fulfilling the Company's obligation to shareholders. McDonald's has and will continue to strive to be a leader in this area. McDonald's Board believes that good governance is a journey, not a destination. Accordingly, they are committed to reviewing McDonald's governance principles at least annually with a view to continuous improvement. One thing that will not change, however, is their commitment to ensuring the integrity of the McDonald's System in all its dealings with stakeholders.

Figure 10: McDonald's Corporate Responsibility

Board Committees

The Audit Committee reviews the performance, and recommends to the Board the selection and retention, of the Company's independent auditors. The Audit Committee reviews with the internal auditors and the independent auditors the overall scope and results of their respective audits, the internal accounting and financial controls and the steps management has taken to monitor and control the Company's major risk exposure.

The Compensation Committee evaluates the performance of the Company's Chief Executive Officer in consultation with the outside Directors and recommends his compensation to the Board annually; reviews and approves senior management's compensation; and establishes compensation guidelines for all other officers. The Committee administers the Company's incentive compensation and stock option plans and develops compensation policies. The Committee has oversight for the detailed disclosure requirements regarding executive compensation.

The Governance Committee sets criteria for Board membership; searches for and screens candidates to fill Board vacancies; recommends appropriate candidates for election each year and, in this regard, evaluates individual Director performance; assesses overall Board performance; considers issues regarding Board composition and size; recommends to the Board the compensation paid to outside Directors; and evaluates the Company's corporate governance process. The Committee also considers and makes recommendations to the Board regarding shareholder proposals for inclusion in the Company's annual Proxy Statement. In addition, under our majority voting standard for uncontested Director elections, if an incumbent Director fails to be re-elected, the Committee is responsible for making a recommendation to the Board about whether to accept the Director's resignation.

The Board also has an Executive Committee and a Finance Committee. The Executive Committee may exercise most Board powers during the period between Board meetings.

The Finance Committee ensures that the Company's significant financial policies and plans, such as its dividend policy and share repurchase program are considered in appropriate detail in light of the Company's overall strategy and performance. The Committee has principal oversight responsibility with respect to certain material financial matters, including the Company's treasury activities, as well as acquisitions and divestitures that are significant to the Company's business. The Committee annually reviews the Company's worldwide insurance program, banking and trading arrangements, and policies with respect to dividends and share repurchase.

The Sustainability and Corporate Responsibility Committee acts in an advisory capacity to the Board of Directors and Company's management with respect to policies and strategies that affect the Company's corporate social responsibilities and its performance as a sustainable organization, including issues pertaining to nutrition and well-being initiatives; supply chain practices; environmental responsibility; employment practices; government relations initiatives; diversity initiatives; marketing and communication practices; philanthropic and community efforts; and other initiatives that may impact McDonald's corporate responsibility and sustainability efforts.

Director Compensation

Management Directors shall not be compensated for their services as Directors. The Governance Committee shall determine the form and amount of compensation for independent Directors, including the non-executive Chairman, if applicable, subject to approval of the full Board of Directors. The Committee shall be sensitive to questions of independence that may be raised where Director Fees and expenses exceed customary levels for companies of comparable scope and size.

The Board of Directors believes that an alignment of Director Interests with those of shareholders is important. All Directors are expected to own stock in the Company in accordance with the policy established by the Governance Committee.

Figure 11: McDonald's Employees Pledge to Abide by the Rules

Generic Industry Type

During the past few years, the Fast Food Restaurants industry experienced a major slowdown due to changing consumer tastes and a struggling economy. Over the five years to 2011, IBIS World expects that industry revenue declined at an average annual rate of 1.6% to $165.4 billion. After revenue declined 4.2% in 2009 to $158.8 billion, it began its upward climb in 2010 with growth of 2.0%. From 2010 to 2011, revenue is expected to have grown an additional 2.1%.

Average consumers are spending less on luxuries like eating out, and when they do, they are purchasing lower-price items. Still, fast-food restaurants are increasingly losing to home-cooked meals in the battle over people's shrinking budgets. Consumers are also becoming increasingly health conscious. While major fast-food retailers have responded by expanding the number of healthy options on their menus, the general trend toward health awareness has hurt the typically greasy Fast Food Restaurants industry. In response to weak market conditions, the number of establishments has stayed flat, increasing only marginally at an average annual rate of 0.1% to 259,788 in the five years to 2011. Industry employment has been flat too, declining at an average rate of 0.7% per year to 3.5 million employee's total.

The long-term trend of major fast-food brands investing in specialty chains and ethnic food chains, such as Mexican food, has remained strong. Many of these operations have grown over the past few years and outperformed the industry as a whole. Major operators, like McDonald's, have expanded their menus to offer nontraditional, high-margin menu items, such as coffee drinks, aiding them in their turnaround. Many major chains are also investing in international growth as part of their long-term strategy. Fast-food restaurants view China in particular as a market that has huge potential for growth and long-term profitability. As such, these trends are expected to contribute to average revenue growth of 2.0% per year to $182.8 billion in the five years to 2016. (IBS World)

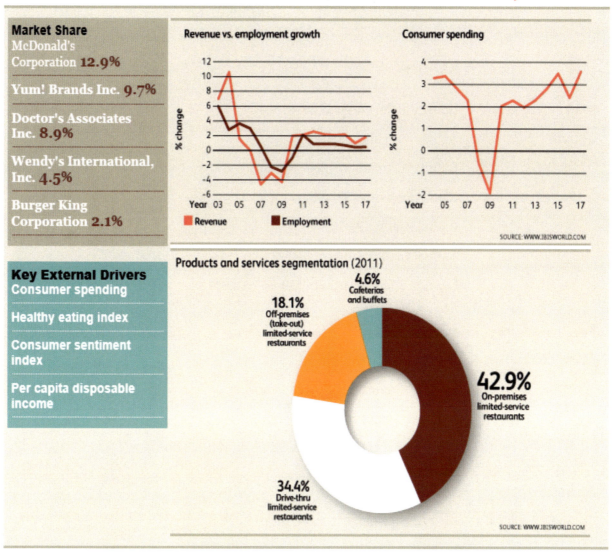

Figure 12: Industry Overview (IBISWorld)

Industry Definition	Fast food restaurants industry is composed of restaurants where patrons pay before eating. Purchases may be consumed on-site, taken out or delivered. Gross sales come from franchises and company-owned stores. This industry specifically excludes coffee and snack shops. Officially reported SEC company revenue (net revenue) refers to revenue obtained only from company-owned stores and franchise fees. Franchised stores' gross sales revenue is not available to the franchisor.
Market Size and Growth	Domestic Revenue: $165.4bn Domestic Profit: $5.5bn Domestic Annual Growth (11-16): 2.0% Global Revenue: $838 bn Global Profit: $25.1bn Annual Global Growth: 3.4% Expected Global Growth (09-14): 18.3%
Key Rivals & Market Share	Key rivals: Yum! Brands, Inc. (9.7%) Doctor's Associates, Inc. (8.9%) Wendy's International, Inc. (4.5%) Burger King Corporation (2.1%) Market share: McDonald's Corporation: 12.9%
Scope of Competitive Rivalry	Competition level: High (heavy price based competition) External competition arises from other food service areas, including full-service restaurants that offer take-out services. There is significant competition among the major franchised companies to obtain suitable sites, which has increased the costs of prime sites. The global foodservice market has defied the global economic downturn and continued to experience growth year on year.
Concentration vs.	Concentration level: Low

Fragmentation	(the top four players account for less than 40.0% of available market share)
Number of Buyers	Every age group and income level eats fast food. Major markets: 64% - households with incomes >$75,000 23.1% - incomes >$50,000 12.9% - incomes from $50,000 to $75,000
Demand Determinants	This industry is sensitive to factors that affect growth in household disposable income, since this is the primary way that consumers finance restaurant and dining expenditure. Household disposable income growth is affected by changes in labor market growth (i.e. unemployment), tax and interest rates and high and increasing gas prices. It is also sensitive to changes in consumer sentiment. The changing age structure of the population is also influencing industry change. The baby boomers (those ages 35 to 55) are a major group affecting revenue growth, since this demographic has the numbers and high disposable income to spend on fast food and restaurant meals. Broken down by age, people from 18 to 25 years old spend 46.4% of their food budget dining out, and people 25 to 30 years old spend 44.8% of their budget dining out. Individuals from 35 to 50 years old spend 42.3% of their food budget dining out, while people 50 to 65 years old spend 42.8% of their budget dining out. People who are 65 or older spend 37.0% of their food budget dining out. US Census household expenditure data indicates that households with incomes of more than $50,000 account for about 77.0% of the total personal expenditure on food eaten away from the home. Of this group, households that earn more than $75,000 a year provide about 64.0% of the total away-from-home food expenditure. Convenience, value for money and time are other important demand determinants. More recently, consumers have become far more health conscious, which is influencing certain quick-service operators. In particular, there are concerns about fat content, fried foods and salt content. There have also been concerns about the quality of meat products

	(related to mad cow disease).
Degree of Product Differentiation	McDonald's decided to become less diversified. To reach this objective, the firm disposed of its interest in the Chipotle Mexican Grill restaurant concept and the Boston Market chain and sold its minority interest in Pret a Manger as well. Operationally, McDonald's started listening carefully to its customers, who were demanding value for their dollars and convenience as well as healthier products. One
Product Innovation	McDonald's decided to focus on product innovations and upgrades of its existing properties instead of continuing to rapidly expand the number of units while relying almost exclusively on the core products it had sold for many years as the source of its sales revenue.
Key Success Factors	**Business expertise of operators** Business expertise is required because this is a high turnover, but low margin industry, with losses easily made. **Having a clear market position** Clear market positioning offers a competitive advantage against competitors in the limited-service industry and other food-service operators. **Effective cost controls** Cost controls are important in this low-margin industry, particularly related to minimizing food waste. **Ability to franchise operations** Franchising both in United States and overseas is now a significant component of this industry and can provide necessary support to owners. **Product is sold at high profile outlets** Having high-profile locations for stores, with easy access, parking and drive-through services increases convenience for customers. **Access to multi-skilled and flexible workforce** Industry operators need access to a good supply of skilled, casual workers to

	meet peak service demand periods.
Supply/Demand Conditions	**Consumer spending** Factors that influence the growth of personal consumption expenditure affect this industry. During a recession, the spike in unemployment generally leads to declines in consumption levels. When personal consumption expenditure is high, consumers will be more likely to spend money on eating out at fast-food restaurants. This driver is expected to increase in 2012, providing a potential opportunity for the industry. **Healthy eating index** The healthy eating index is expected to decrease slowly in 2012 as consumers' diets continue to become progressively poorer. Still, consumers are also becoming increasingly aware of issues related to weight and obesity, fatty-food intake and food safety issues. This factor particularly affects the often meaty and greasy fast-food industry. Despite any long-term aggregate declines in healthy eating, consumers are now more aware of the health issues associated with fatty foods and are increasingly going out of their way to avoid them. This is a potential threat for the industry **Per capita disposable income** The industry is affected by factors that influence the growth in household disposable income, including changes to tax and interest rates and changes in labor market growth. During an economic recession, the spike in unemployment leads to more subdued growth in household incomes. High and increasing gas prices also adversely affect disposable income, decreasing consumer expenditure on take-out food. This driver is expected to increase slowly in 2012. **Consumer sentiment index** Changes in consumer sentiment have a large effect on household expenditure on discretionary items, including fast-food. During a recession, demand for lower-priced value products from fast food restaurants increases.

Global foodservice industry value: $ billion, 2005–09

Year	$ billion	€ billion	% Growth
2005	694.0	499.1	
2006	731.0	525.7	5.3%
2007	774.1	556.7	5.9%
2008	810.8	583.1	4.7%
2009	838.0	602.7	3.4%

CAGR: 2005–09   4.8%

Source: Datamonitor   DATAMONITOR

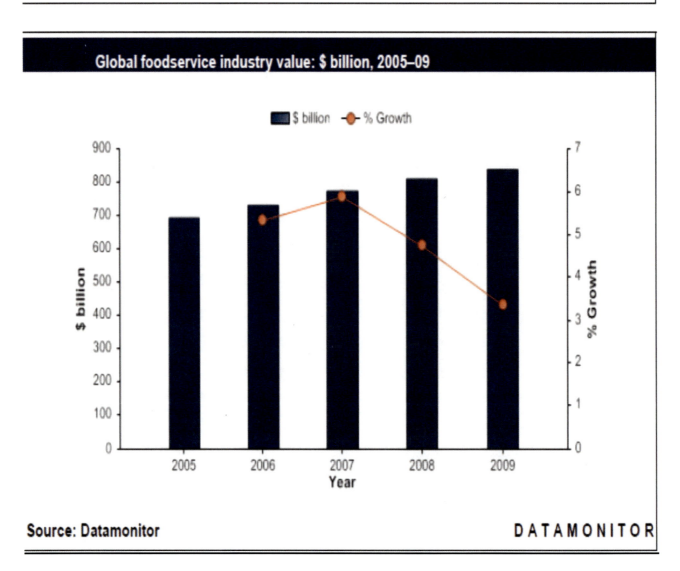

Global foodservice industry value: $ billion, 2005–09

Source: Datamonitor   DATAMONITOR

Figure 13: Global Foodservice Industry (Datamonitor)

Organizational Structure

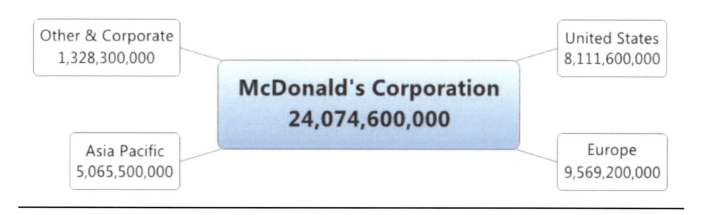

Figure 14: McDonald's Organization Structure

Organizational structure is defined as a relatively stable arrangement of responsibilities, tasks, and people within an organization. Organizations are composed of people who are assigned to certain divisions and who perform certain delegated and specialized tasks. The structure of an organization, therefore, is a framework that management has devised to divide tasks, deploy resources, and coordinate departments. Structure provides a way for information to flow efficiently from people and departments who generate it to those who need it. Structure also spells out decisions rights- policies that tell individuals who's responsible for generating particular information and who's authorized to act on it.

The structure includes a firm's authority hierarchy, its organizational units and divisions, and its mechanisms for coordinating internal activities. Organizational structure performs two essential functions: it ensures control, and coordinates information, decisions, and the activities of employees at all levels. As both functions become more complex, firms generally modify their structure accordingly. Structure should be consistent with the firm's strategy. The more diversified the firm, the more structure that will have to be designed to accommodate coordination. After all, if a firm is participating is related business; it is probably trying to exploit synergies, and often requires sharing information and resources across product or geographic divisions. Conversely, the more focused the form is on a single business; the more its structure should be designed to emphasize control.

McDonald's operates under the international strategy, and focuses on adjusting their products based on cultural differences around the world. The international strategy is based on core competencies, which is a basis for competitive advantage. The strategy is company based, and is the same all over the world.

McDonald's operates under the matrix structure. Matrix structure is a form of organization in which specialists from functional departments are assigned to work for one or more product or geographic units. The matric structure is designed to take advantage of the benefits of both basic forms- functional specialization and divisional autonomy. Matrix provides flexibility by making it possible to organize teams around specific projects, products, or markets. The utility of a matrix structure increases when the pressures facing a firm are unpredictable and require both high degrees of control and extensive coordination of resources. Many firms find it difficult to implement the matrix structure because it calls for high levels ort resources sharing across divisions; in fact, it's generally feasible only when strong culture and shared values support cross-division collaborations.

Strategic Advantages	Strategic Disadvantages
- Gives formal attention to each dimension of strategic priority - Creates checks and balances among competing viewpoints - Facilitates capture of functionally based strategic fits in diversified companies - Promotes making trade-off decisions on the basis of "what's best for the organization as a whole" - Encourages cooperation, consensus-building, conflict resolution, and coordination of related activates	- Very complex to manage - Hard to maintain "balance" between the two lines of authority - So much shared authority can result in a transactions logjam and disproportionate amounts of time being spent on communications, consensus building, and collaboration - Promotes organizational bureaucracy and hamstrings creative entrepreneurship and initiative - Works at cross purposes with efforts to empower down-the-line managers and employees

Financial Analysis

Graphs

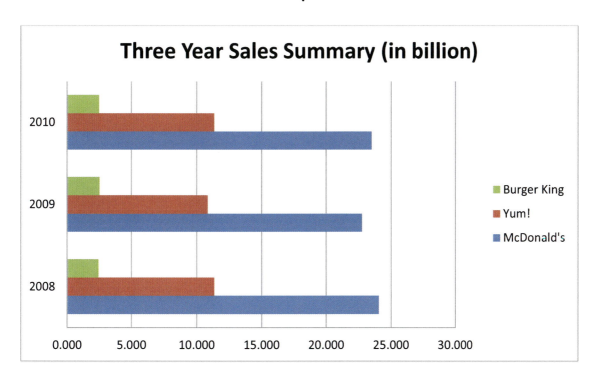

Three Year Sales	McDonald's	Yum!	Burger King
2008	24.075	11.343	2.455
2009	22.745	10.836	2.537
2010	23.522	11.343	2.502

The graph shows McDonald's and its two competitors: Burger King and Yum Brand's sales for the last three years. McDonald's is a definitely leader in sales over the past three years.

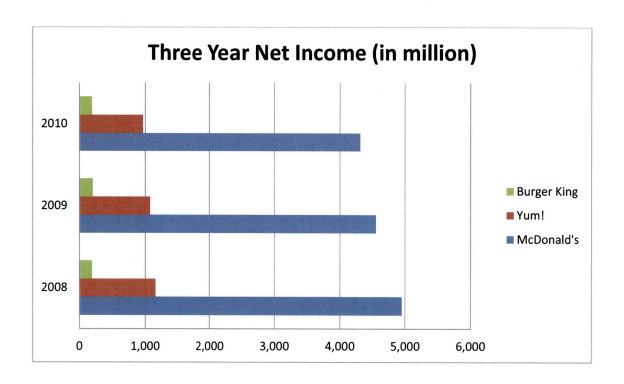

Three Years Net Income (in millions)	McDonald's	Yum!	Burger King
2008	4,946	1,158	187
2009	4,551	1,071	200
2010	4,313	964	190

The graph shows McDonald's and its two competitors: Burger King and Yum Brand's net income for the last three years. McDonald's proves to be a leader in net income compared with the competitors.

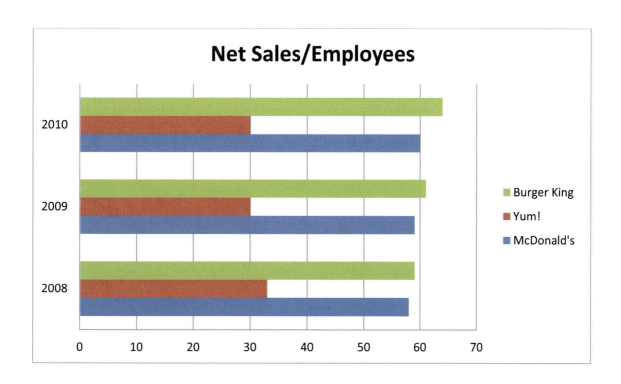

Net Sales/Employees	McDonald's	Yum!	Burger King
2008	58	33	59
2009	59	30	61
2010	60	30	64

The net sales per employee ration measures employee productivity. The sales per employee metric are a good measure of personnel productivity, with its greatest use being the comparison of industry competitors and the historical performance of the company.

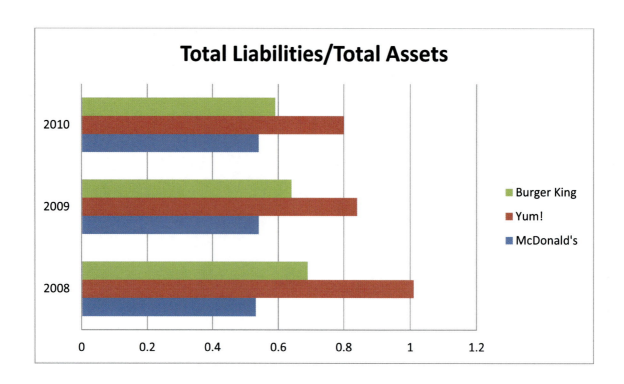

Total Liabilities/Total Assets	McDonald's	Yum!	Burger King
2008	0.53	1.01	0.69
2009	0.54	0.84	0.64
2010	0.54	0.8	0.59

Total liabilities to total assets ratio is a metric used to measure a company's financial risk by determining how much of the company's assets have been financed by debt. It is calculated by adding short-term and long-term debt and then dividing by the company's total assets. This is a very broad ratio as it includes short- and long-term debt as well as all types of both tangible and intangible assets.

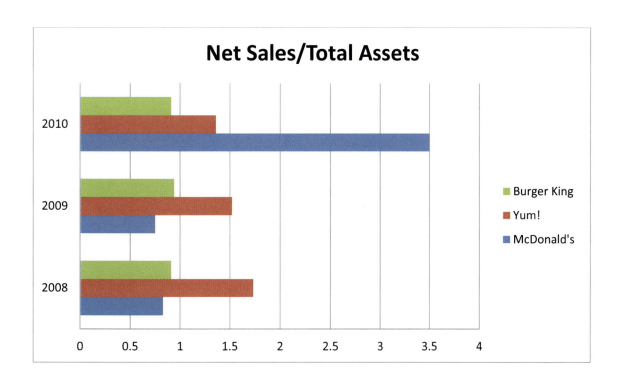

Net Sales/Total Assets	McDonald's	Yum!	Burger King
2008	0.83	1.73	0.91
2009	0.75	1.52	0.94
2010	3.5	1.36	0.91

Sales to total assets ratio is called an asset turnover ratio. It is the amount of sales generated for every dollar's worth of assets. It is calculated by dividing sales in dollars by assets in dollars. Asset turnover measures a firm's efficiency at using its assets in generating sales or revenue - the higher the number the better. It also indicates pricing strategy: companies with low profit margins tend to have high asset turnover, while those with high profit margins have low asset turnover. This ratio usually varies even more than most of the other ratios by industry. In 2010, McDonald's asset turnover was as high as 3.5, and was the largest out of the competitors.

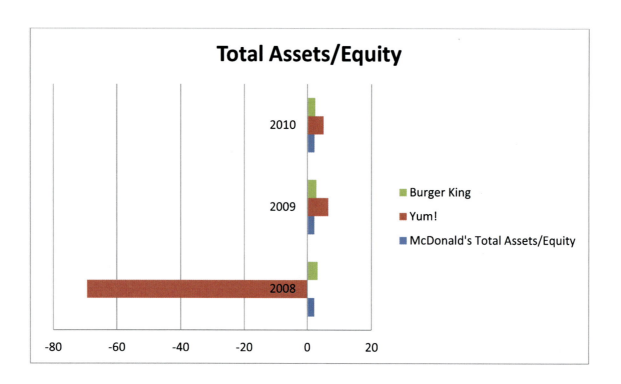

Total Assets/Equity	McDonald's	Yum!	Burger King
2008	2.13	-69.44	3.18
2009	2.15	6.42	2.78
2010	2.18	4.98	2.43

Total assets over equity ratio are often used as a measure of leverage. Leverage is a degree to which an investor or business is utilizing borrowed money. Companies that are highly leveraged may be at risk of bankruptcy if they are unable to make payments on their debt, they may also be unable to find new lenders in the future. Leverage is not always bad, however, it can increase the shareholder's return on investment and often there is tax advantages associated with borrowing. McDonald's seems to have a steady level of leverage, so it gains trust over the competitors, such as Yum Brands that had a large negative leverage in 2008.

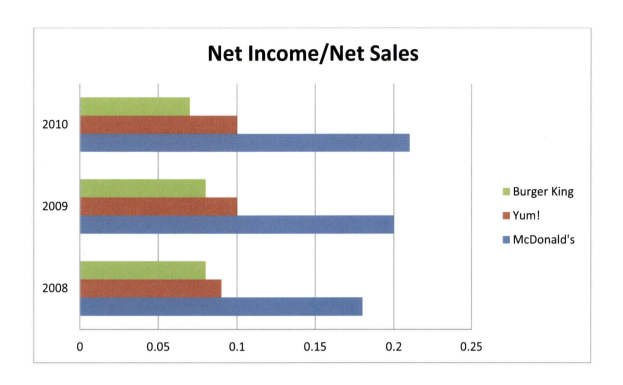

Net Income/Net Sales	McDonald's	Yum!	Burger King
2008	0.18	0.09	0.08
2009	0.2	0.1	0.08
2010	0.21	0.1	0.07

A ratio of profitability calculated as net income divided by revenues, or net profits divided by sales, and is also known as net profit margin. It measures how much out of every dollar of sales a company actually keeps in earnings.

Profit margin is very useful when comparing companies in similar industries. A higher profit margin indicates a more profitable company that has better control over its costs compared to its competitors. Profit margin is displayed as a percentage; a 20% profit margin, for example, means the company has a net income of $0.20 for each dollar of sales. McDonald's proved to have a highest profitability when compared to its competitors.

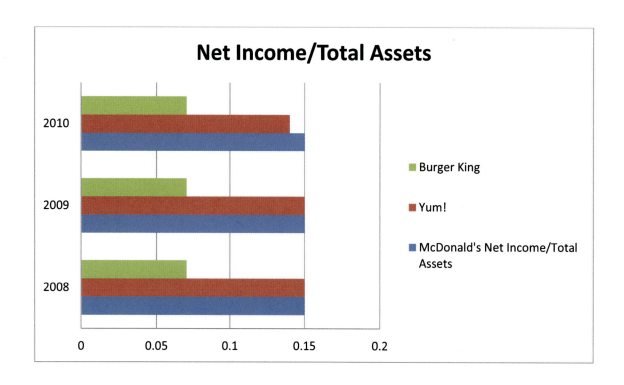

Net Income/Total Assets	McDonald's	Yum!	Burger King
2008	0.15	0.15	0.07
2009	0.15	0.15	0.07
2010	0.15	0.14	0.07

Net income over total assets is called a Return on Assets ratio. An indicator of how profitable a company is relative to its total assets. ROA gives an idea as to how efficient management is at using its assets to generate earnings. Calculated by dividing a company's annual earnings by its total assets, ROA is displayed as a percentage. Sometimes this is referred to as "return on investment".

ROA tells you what earnings were generated from invested capital (assets). ROA for public companies can vary substantially and will be highly dependent on the industry. This is why when using ROA as a comparative measure, it is best to compare it against a company's previous ROA numbers or the ROA of a similar company.

As it is shown on the graph above, McDonald's ROA are 15 percent, which is the same like Yum Brand's ROA, while Burger King only has 7 percent of ROA.

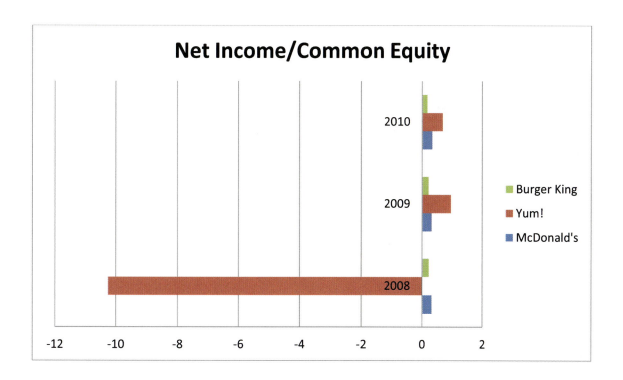

Net Income/Common Equity	McDonald's	Yum!	Burger King
2008	0.32	-10.26	0.22
2009	0.32	0.96	0.21
2010	0.34	0.69	0.17

The net income over common equity ratio is known as Return on Equity ratio that is the amount of net income returned as a percentage of shareholders equity. Return on equity measures a corporation's profitability by revealing how much profit a company generates with the money shareholders have invested.

Net income is for the full fiscal year (before dividends paid to common stock holders but after dividends to preferred stock.) Shareholder's equity does not include preferred shares. The ROE is useful for comparing the profitability of a company to that of other firms in the same industry.

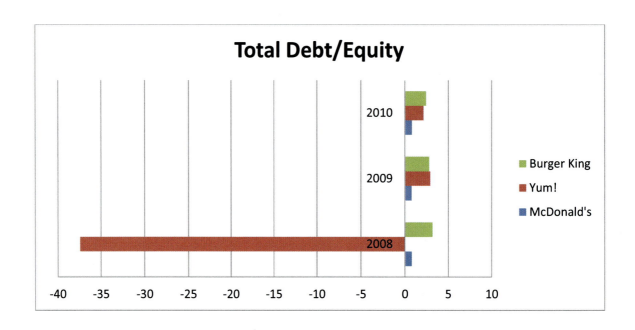

Total Debt/Equity	McDonald's	Yum!	Burger King
2008	0.76	-37.45	3.18
2009	0.75	2.9	2.78
2010	0.79	2.13	2.43

Total debt over equity ratio is a measure of a company's financial leverage calculated by dividing its total liabilities by stockholders' equity. It indicates what proportion of equity and debt the company is using to finance its assets.

A high debt/equity ratio generally means that a company has been aggressive in financing its growth with debt. This can result in volatile earnings as a result of the additional interest expense. If a lot of debt is used to finance increased operations (high debt to equity), the company could potentially generate more earnings than it would have without this outside financing. If this were to increase earnings by a greater amount than the debt cost (interest), then the shareholders benefit as more earnings are being spread among the same amount of shareholders. However, the cost of this debt financing may outweigh the return that the company generates on the debt through investment and business activities and become too much for the company to handle. This can lead to bankruptcy, which would leave shareholders with nothing.

The debt/equity ratio also depends on the industry in which the company operates. For example, capital-intensive industries such as auto manufacturing tend to have a debt/equity ratio above 2, while personal computer companies have a debt/equity of under 0.5.

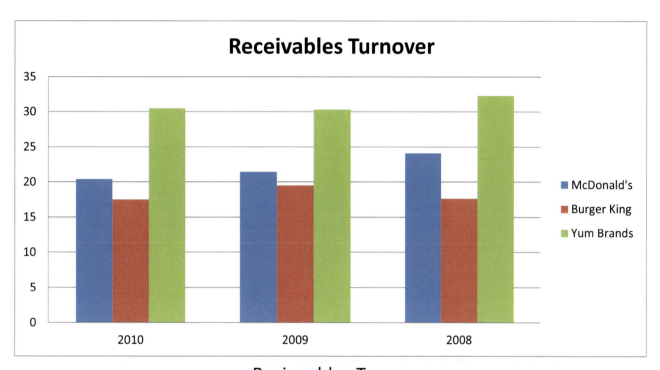

Recievables Turnover

	McDonald's	Burger King	Yum Brands
2010	20.42	17.51	30.49
2009	21.45	19.52	30.35
2008	24.13	17.66	32.3

By dividing the cost of sales over the course of a year by the average inventory for the same period, it is possible to determine how fast a firm moves inventory. In some industries credit and collection policies have a significant impact on both sales and cash flow. A relatively low ratio here indicated either that credit policies are too lenient or that collections are inefficient. In such a case, check for the bad debt expense if possible. A low accounts receivable turnover and an unfavorable inventory turnover are an especially difficult combination. A relatively high ratio might mean that credit policies are too strict, and that sales are being lost as a result. As we can tell McDonald's receivable turnover has been slightly decreasing over the past 3 years by an average of 2%.

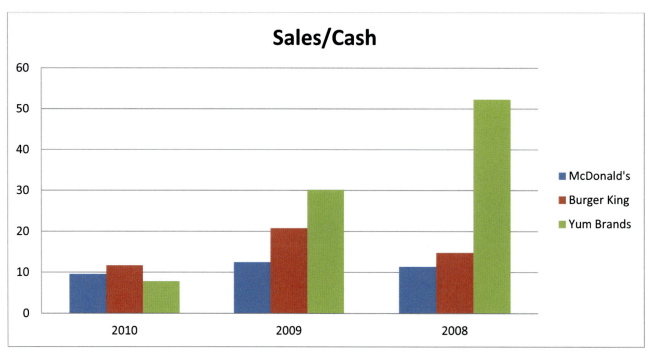

	Sales/Cash		
	McDonald's	Burger King	Yum Brands
2010	9.61	11.72	7.87
2009	12.5	20.8	30.18
2008	11.4	14.79	52.33

Comparison of cash balance at the end of a period (usually expressed in number of weeks or months) to the sales revenue in that period. It indicates the effectiveness of the firm's credit and collection policies, and the amount of cash required as buffer for unexpected delays in cash collection. It is the inverse of cash turnover ratio. This shows that McDonald's Corporation through the years is becoming more effective in collecting credit; showing that their cash collection policies are working successfully and listening to the needs of not only McDonald's Corporation but also its franchises.

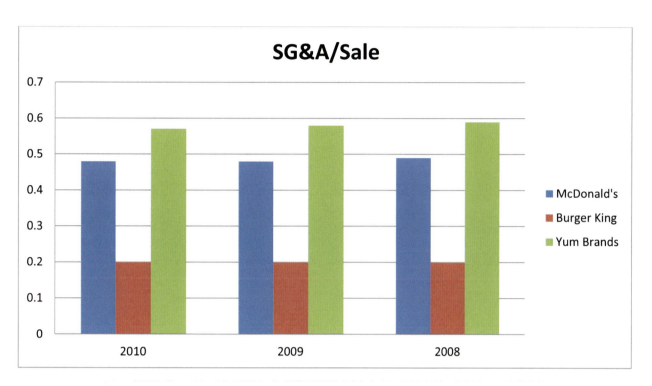

SG&A/ Sales

	McDonald's	Burger King	Yum Brands
2010	0.48	0.2	0.57
2009	0.48	0.2	0.58
2008	0.49	0.2	0.59

    SG&A to Sales is the ratio of selling, general and administrative costs to sales. Selling, general, and administrative (SG&A) expenses represent most operating expenses including marketing costs, employee salaries, pension costs, insurance, etc. When determining SG&A/Sales ratios we need to look for a steady or decreasing percentage indicating that the company is controlling its overhead expenses. Looking at the graph one can tell that McDonald's Corporation is doing an effective job by keeping its ratio decreasing and steady through the last 3 years. The same goes for its competitors as well. Though in comparison to its competitors, McDonald's Corporation does not have the most efficient ratio and thus needs to keep striving for better opportunity in this area in order to obtain greater profit.

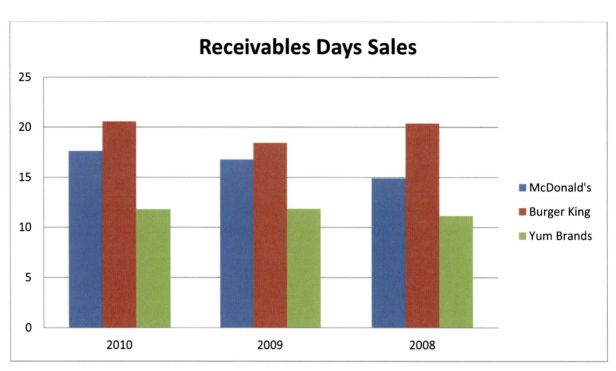

Receivables Days Sales			
	McDonald's	Burger King	Yum Brands
2010	17.63	20.56	11.81
2009	16.78	18.44	11.86
2008	14.92	20.38	11.15

    This calculation shows the average number of days it takes to collect your accounts receivable (number of days of sales in receivables). In this ratio we are looking for trends that indicate a change in your customers' payment habits. Compare the calculated days in receivables to your stated terms. Compare to industry standards. Review an Aging of Receivables and be familiar with your customer's payment habits and watch for any changes that might indicate a problem. Due to the high importance of cash in running a business, it is in a company's best interest to collect outstanding receivables as quickly as possible. By quickly turning sales into cash, a company has the chance to put the cash to use again - ideally, to reinvest and make more sales. This ratio can be used to determine whether a company is trying to disguise weak sales, or is generally being ineffective at bringing money in. For most businesses, this ratio is looked at either quarterly or annually. Looking at the graph we see that McDonald's Corporation is becoming more ineffective with each passing year, thus making taking it looking to turn a profit.

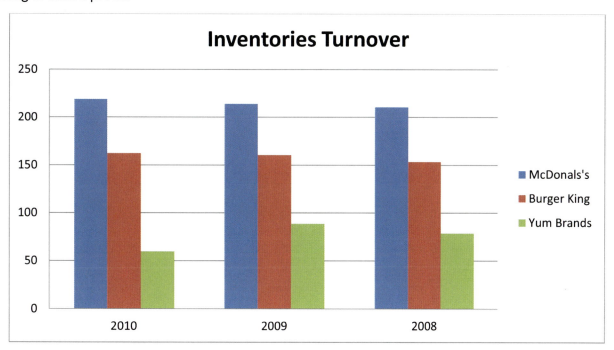

Inventories Turnover			
	McDonals's	Burger King	Yum Brands
2010	219.06	162.48	60.02
2009	214.17	160.59	88.82
2008	210.96	153.44	79.05

This ratio determines the number of times that you turn over (or sell) inventory during the year. Generally, a high inventory turnover is an indicator of good inventory management. But a high ratio can also mean there is a shortage of inventory. A low turnover may indicate overstocking, or obsolete inventory. Compare to industry standards. Since McDonald's Corporation's inventory levels are increasing, it can be seen as unhealthy because it represents an investment with a rate of zero. It also opens the company up to trouble should prices begin to fall. These rising levels could also mean strong sales or ineffective buying.

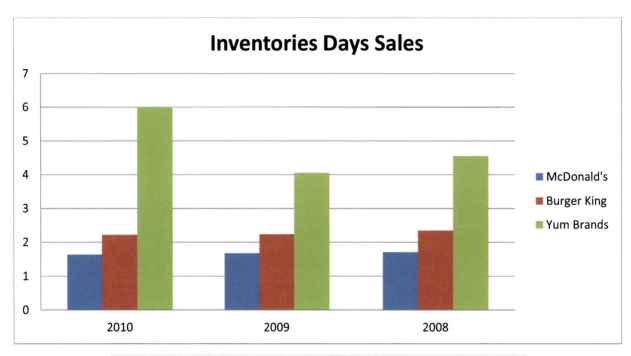

Inventories Days Sales			
	McDonald's	Burger King	Yum Brands
2010	1.64	2.22	6
2009	1.68	2.24	4.05
2008	1.71	2.35	4.55

    This ratio is a financial measure of a company's performance that gives investors an idea of how long it takes a company to turn its inventory (including goods that are work in progress, if applicable) into sales. Generally, the lower (shorter) ratio the better, but it is important to note that the average varies from one industry to another. This measure is one part of the cash conversion cycle, which represents the process of turning raw materials into cash. The day's sales of inventory are the first stage in that process. The other two stages are day's sales outstanding and day's payable outstanding. The first measures how long it takes a company to receive payment on accounts receivable, while the second measures how long it takes a company to pay off its accounts payable. Since the McDonald's Corporation primarily works with food items it has a lower ration, turning its inventory into cash extremely quick compared to its two competitors.

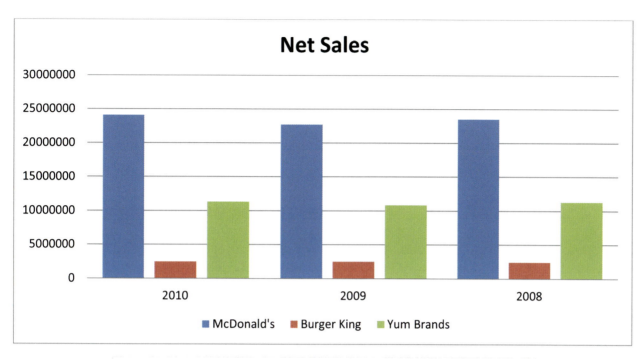

Net Sales			
	McDonald's	Burger King	Yum Brands
2010	24074600	2502200	11343000
2009	22744700	2537400	10836000
2008	23522400	2455000	11304000

    This ratio shows the amount of sales generated by a company after the deduction of returns, allowances for damaged or missing goods and any discounts allowed. The sales number reported on a company's financial statements is a net sales number, reflecting these deductions. Deductions from the gross sales are represented in the net sales figure. Therefore, a net sale gives a more accurate picture of the actual sales generated by the company, or the money that it expects to receive. A company will book its revenue once the good or service is delivered or performed for the customer. However, in the case of returns, even after a good has been sold it can often be returned under a company's return policy. If the good is returned by the customer, it is not considered a sale, as the customer will receive a credit or money back, so it needs to be deducted from the gross sales. The allowances for damaged or missing goods reflect the situations in which the goods are damaged in transit or are not what the customer expected. Many companies also offer discounts, especially on credit sales where the customer pays off the amount early. This discount is deducted from gross sales, reducing overall revenue. Compared to its two competitors, McDonald's Corporation has the least amount of Net Sales. This shows that there sales is not sufficient enough and thus must be modified in order to increase profit.

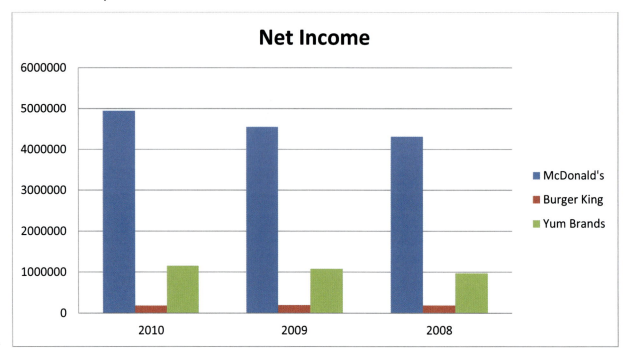

Net Income			
	McDonald's	Burger King	Yum Brands
2010	4946300	186800	1158000
2009	4551000	200100	1083000
2008	4313200	190000	972000

This ratio is a company's total earnings (or profit). Net income is calculated by taking revenues and adjusting for the cost of doing business, depreciation, interest, taxes and other expenses. This number is found on a company's income statement and is an important measure of how profitable the company is over a period of time. The measure is also used to calculate earnings per share. Often referred to as "the bottom line" since net income is listed at the bottom of the income statement. When basing an investment decision on net income numbers, it is important to review the quality of the numbers that were used to arrive at this value. Overall, McDonald's Corporations' net income is doubled compared to its competitors and thus is seen as a great investment.

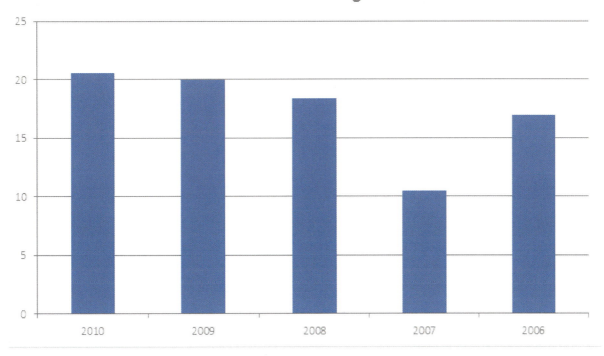

Net Income as a Percentage of Net Sales

To maintain this growth the McDonald's Corporation and its execution of the strategic plan are part of the Plan to Win, which is subject to risks. The most important of these is whether we can remain relevant to our customers and a brand they trust. Meeting customer expectations is complicated by the risks inherent in our global operating environment. The IEO segment of the restaurant industry, although largely mature in our major markets, is highly fragmented and competitive. The IEO segment has been contracting in many markets, including some major markets, due to unfavorable economic conditions, and this may continue. Persistently high unemployment rates in many markets have also increased consumer focus on value and heightened pricing sensitivity. Combined with increasing pressure on commodity and labor costs, these circumstances affect restaurant sales and margin growth despite the strength of our brand and value proposition. We have the added challenge of the cultural, economic and regulatory differences that exist within and among the more than 100 countries where we operate. Initiatives we undertake may not have universal appeal among different segments of our customer base and can drive unanticipated changes in guest counts and customer perceptions. Our operations, plans and results are also affected by regulatory and similar initiatives around the world, notably the focus on nutritional content and the production, processing and preparation of food "from field to front counter," as well as industry marketing practices." (McDonalds.com)

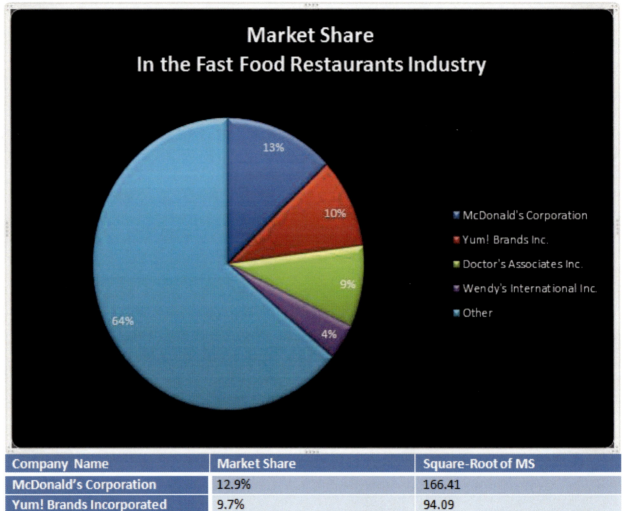

Company Name	Market Share	Square-Root of MS
McDonald's Corporation	12.9%	166.41
Yum! Brands Incorporated	9.7%	94.09
Doctor's Associates Inc.	8.9%	79.21
Wendy's International Inc.	4.5%	24.01
Total	36	363.72

    The fast food restaurants industry is a fragmented industry, an industry which contains many small or relatively small competitors. This industry has no, or few, leaders in each relevant geographic and/or product market. The four biggest companies in the industry combine for less than 50% of the market share leaving 64% of the market share for many other small companies

    As one can observe from the table and the chart above, McDonald's leads the industry with the highest market share of almost 13%. However, the next three big competitors are not far behind. Thus to continuously stay ahead of the curve McDonald's Corporation must make sure to true its threats into opportunities.

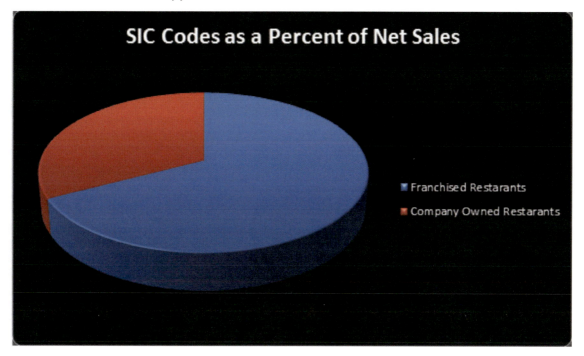

McDonald's Corporation is working hard to keep up their profit and sales. Their strategy of market development is working and is keeping the company strong so far. With its constant growth means that over the years McDonald's has had a variety of other expenses and expenditures that are taking a margin out of the total Net Profit. However, the company is still doing very well and remains the market leader.

Altman's Z-Score for 2010

The Altman Z-Score is a measure of overall, day-to-day company health. It is the sum of five key financial ratios, of which each ratio is multiplied by a predetermined weight factor. Results below 1.81 indicate that the company may be heading towards bankruptcy.

Z = 1.2A + 1.4B + 3.3C + 0.6D + 0.99E

A = Working capital/total assets = 1,443,800/31,384,800= 0.046

B = Retained earnings/total assets = 33,811,700/31,384,800= 1.077

C = Earnings before interest and taxes/total assets = 7,288,400/31,384,800= 0.232

D = Market value of equity/book value of total debt = 97,720,232/16,750,600= 5.834

E = Sales/total assets = 24,074,600/31,384,800= 0.767

McDonald's Z-Score is: 6.5964

If Z-score is above 2.99, the company is in good shape.

Tobin's Q Ratio

Tobin's Q examines a company's Market Price per share to Book Value per share. If the result of dividing Market by Book Value is near the Book Value per share than the company's Market Price per share is legitimized.

The Q ratio is calculated as the market value of a company divided by the replacement value of the firm's assets:

$$Q\ Ratio = \frac{Total\ Market\ Value\ of\ Firm}{Total\ Asset\ Value}$$

A low Q (between 0 and 1) means that the cost to replace a firm's assets is greater than the value of its stock. This implies that the stock is undervalued. Conversely, a high Q (greater than 1) implies that a firm's stock is more expensive than the replacement cost of its assets, which implies that the stock is overvalued. This measure of stock valuation is the driving factor behind investment decisions in Tobin's model.

McDonald's Q Ratio = 80,874,336,000/31,384,800,000= 2.57, which means that the stocks of McDonald's are overvalued.

McDonald's Corporation – Du Pont Chart 2010

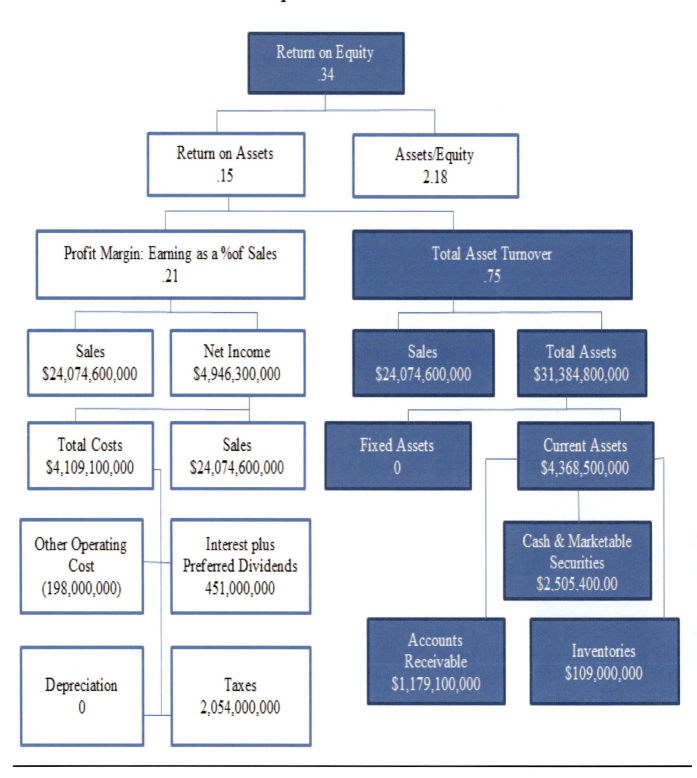

Figure 15: McDonald's Corporation Du Pont Analysis 2010

S.W.O.T. Analysis

- **Strengths**
    - Strong brand value sustains the company's leadership position
    - Operates 32,737 restaurants in 117 countries
    - McDonald's strong brand recognition enables company to expand its markets
    - Company serves 64 million customers per day
    - McDonald's is ranked number one in food service category in Fortune's 2010 list of World's Most Admired Companies
    - McDonald's revenues have grown with an increase in global market share, and sales increased by 5% in 2010
    - Diversified geographic presence increased opportunities in emerging markets
    - Revenues from outside US are about 66.3% of the company's total revenues.
    - Revenues from Asia/Pacific, Middle East and Africa increased 16.8% in 2010
    - Total revenues in 2010 were $24,074.6 million and are the highest amongst the competitors
    - McDonald's is a leader in operating margins, which were at 31.04% in 2010 compared to its competitors, such as Yum! Brands at 18.08% and Burger King at 13.3%

- **Weaknesses**
    - Legal proceedings affect brand image adversely, includes violations of consumer fraud acts, unfair competition, strict liability, failure to warn, unjust enrichment, false advertisement and more.
    - Number of product failures, such as Arch Deluxe, McLean Deluxe, McSoup, McPizza, which reflects of poor company's consumer research and branding strategies, and vast of 12 million glassware in 2010 because of high cadmium contents, which recalled company's failure to successfully launch new product line.

- **Opportunities**
    - Growth of franchisee operated restaurants, where the percentage of franchised restaurants worldwide increased from 73.7% in 2006 to 80.4% in 2010
    - The transition to franchisees and developmental license structure is likely to increase profitability of McDonald's
    - Positive outlook for out-of-home eating market can boost top line in long run with investments such as McCafe specialty coffee menu and new premium products such as Angus third Pounder.
    - Growing drinks market is projected to increase the anticipated compounded annual growth rate of 3.7% for the years 2009-2014, which would lead the market to a value of $81.4 billion by the end of 2014

- **Threats**
    - Inflation
    - In 2011 prices in the US have risen by 2%-3%, so McDonald's have to raise prices by the same percentage to offset higher food costs which would reduce the popularity based on low-priced foods
    - Intense competition in retail food industry is increasing due to new product development, price, advertising levels, customer service, reputation, restaurant location, and attractiveness of properties
    - Growing consumer demand for healthy food products, which increases competition with healthy food products companies, such as Subway, which is one of the fastest growing franchises that operates approximately 34,497 restaurants in 98 countries

II. Focal Points for Action

(The following information has been obtained from McDonald's CORP Form 10K)

There are many possible problems and issues which need to be resolved by the McDonald's Corporation in order to stay competitive, successful, and profitable in the fast food industry. Meeting customer expectations is complicated by the risks inherent in our global operating environment. These risks can have an impact both in the near- and long-term and are reflected in the following considerations and factors that we believe are most likely to affect McDonald's performance.

Ability to remain a relevant and trusted brand and to increase sales and profits depends largely on how well the Plan to Win is executed.

The Plan to Win addresses the key drivers of McDonald's business and results—people, products, place, price and promotion. The quality of company's execution depends mainly on the following:

- Ability to anticipate and respond effectively to trends or other factors that affect the IEO segment and competitive position in the diverse markets McDonald's serves, such as spending patterns, demographic changes, trends in food preparation, consumer preferences and publicity about us, all of which can drive popular perceptions of the business or affect the willingness of other companies to enter into site, supply or other arrangements or alliances with McDonald's;

- The risks associated with McDonald's franchise business model, including whether the franchisees and developmental licensees will have the experience and financial resources to be effective operators and remain aligned with McDonald's on operating, promotional and capital-intensive initiatives and the potential impact on us if they experience food safety or other operational problems or project a brand image inconsistent with McDonald's values, particularly if contractual and other rights and remedies are limited by local law or otherwise, costly to exercise or subject to litigation;

- Ability to drive restaurant improvements that achieve optimal capacity, particularly during peak mealtime hours, and to motivate restaurant personnel and its franchisees to achieve consistency and high service levels so as to improve consumer perceptions of McDonald's ability to meet expectations for quality food served in clean and friendly environments;

- The costs and operational risks associated with increasing reliance on information technology (including point-of-sale and other in-store technology systems or platforms), including the risk that McDonald's will not realize fully the benefits of its investments in technology, which McDonald's is accelerating, as well as the potential for system failures, programming errors or breaches of security involving its systems or those of third-party operators of its systems;

- Ability to respond effectively to adverse perceptions about the quick-service category of the IEO segment or about McDonald's products (including their nutritional content), promotions and premiums, such as Happy Meals (collectively, its products), how McDonald's sources the commodities it uses, and its ability to manage the potential impact on McDonald's of food-borne illnesses or product safety issues;

Results and financial condition are affected by global and local market conditions, which can adversely affect McDonald's sales, margins and net income.

Results of operations are substantially affected not only by global economic conditions, but also by local operating and economic conditions, which can vary substantially by market. The key factors that can affect our operations, plans and results in this environment are the following:

- Whether McDonald's strategies will be effective in enabling the continued market share gains that it has included in its plans, while at the same time enabling the company to achieve its targeted operating income growth, despite the uncertain economic outlook, resurgent competitors and a more costly and competitive advertising environment;

- The effectiveness of supply chain management to assure reliable and sufficient product supply on favorable terms;

- The impact on consumer disposable income levels and spending habits of governmental actions to manage national economic matters, whether through austerity or stimulus measures and initiatives intended to control wages, unemployment, credit availability, inflation, taxation and other economic drivers;

- The impact on restaurant sales and margins of recent volatility in commodity and gasoline prices, which McDonald's expects will continue and may be exacerbated by current events in the Middle East, and the impact of pricing, hedging and other actions that we, franchisees and suppliers may take to address this environment;

- The impact on margins of labor costs given our labor-intensive business model, the long-term trend toward higher wages in both mature and developing markets and any potential impact of union organizing efforts;
- The impact of foreign exchange and interest rates on McDonald's financial condition and results;
- The challenges and uncertainties associated with operating in developing markets, which may entail a relatively higher risk of political instability, economic volatility, crime, corruption and social and ethnic unrest, all of which are exacerbated in many cases by a lack of an independent and experienced judiciary and uncertainties in how local law is applied and enforced, including in areas most relevant to commercial transactions and foreign investment;
- The nature and timing of decisions about underperforming markets or assets, including decisions that result in impairment charges that reduce earnings;
- The impact of changes in McDonald's debt levels on its credit ratings, interest expense, and availability of acceptable counterparties, ability to obtain funding on favorable terms or our operating or financial flexibility, especially if lenders impose new operating or financial covenants.

Increasing legal and regulatory complexity will continue to affect our operations and results in material ways.

Legal and regulatory environment worldwide exposes McDonald's to complex compliance, litigation and similar risks that affect its operations and results in material ways.

In many of its markets, including the United States and Europe, McDonald's is subject to increasing regulation, which has increased cost of doing business. In developing markets, McDonald's face the risks associated with new and untested laws and judicial systems. Among the more important regulatory and litigation risks McDonald's faces and must manage are the following:

- The cost, compliance and other risks associated with the often conflicting and highly prescriptive regulations McDonald's faces, especially in the United States where inconsistent standards imposed by local, state and federal authorities can adversely affect popular perceptions of the business and increase exposure to litigation or governmental investigations or proceedings;
- The impact of new, potential or changing regulation that can affect McDonald's business plans, such as those relating to marketing and the content and safety of our food and other products, as well as the risks and costs of our labeling and other disclosure practices, particularly given varying legal requirements and practices for testing and disclosure within the industry, ordinary variations in food

preparation among McDonald's restaurants, and the need to rely on the accuracy and completeness of information from third-party suppliers;

- The impact of nutritional, health and other scientific inquiries and conclusions, which constantly evolve and often have contradictory implications, but nonetheless drive popular opinion, litigation and regulation, including taxation, in ways that could be material to our business;

The trading volatility and price of McDonald's common stock may be affected by many different factors.

Many factors affect the volatility and price of the common stock in addition to McDonald's operating results and prospects.

The most important of these, some of which are outside company's control, are the following:

- Governmental action or inaction in light of key indicators of economic activity or events that can significantly influence financial markets, particularly in the United States which is the principal trading market for McDonald's common stock, and media reports and commentary about economic or other matters, even when the matter in question does not directly relate to the business;
- The impact of McDonald's stock repurchase program or dividend rate;
- The impact on McDonald's results of other corporate actions, such as those the company may take from time to time as part of its continuous review of its corporate structure in light of business, legal and tax considerations.

Results and prospects can be adversely affected by events such as severe weather conditions, natural disasters, hostilities and social unrest, among others.

Severe weather conditions, natural disasters, hostilities and social unrest, terrorist activities, health epidemics or pandemics (or expectations about them) can adversely affect consumer spending and confidence levels or other factors that affect McDonald's results and prospects, such as commodity costs. Company's receipt of proceeds under any insurance it maintains with respect to certain of these risks may be delayed or the proceeds may be insufficient to offset our losses fully.

III. Developing Alternatives

Generic Industry Type & Industry Characteristics

The fast food restaurants industry is composed of restaurants where patrons pay before eating. Purchases may be consumed on-site, taken out or delivered. Gross sales come from franchises and company-owned stores.

Figure 16: Cartoon Figure of McDonald's Food

Main Activities

Primary activities of this industry

Operating drive-thru and take-out facilities
Operating fast-food services
Operating quick-service restaurants

Major products and services in this industry

Cafeterias and buffets
Drive-thru limited-service restaurants
Off-premises (take-out) limited-service restaurants

The Boston Consulting Group Matrix (BCG)

The BCG matrix is a chart that had been created by Bruce Henderson for the Boston Consulting Group in 1968 to help corporations with analyzing their business units or product lines. This helps the company allocate resources and is used as an analytical tool in brand marketing, product management, strategic management, and portfolio analysis

The BCG matrix considers two variables:

Market growth rate

Relative market share

The market growth rate is shown on the vertical (y) axis and is expressed as a %. The range is set somewhat arbitrarily. The overhead shows a range of 0 to 20% with division between low and high growth at 10%.

The horizontal (x) axis shows relative market share. The share is calculated by reference to the largest competitor in the market.

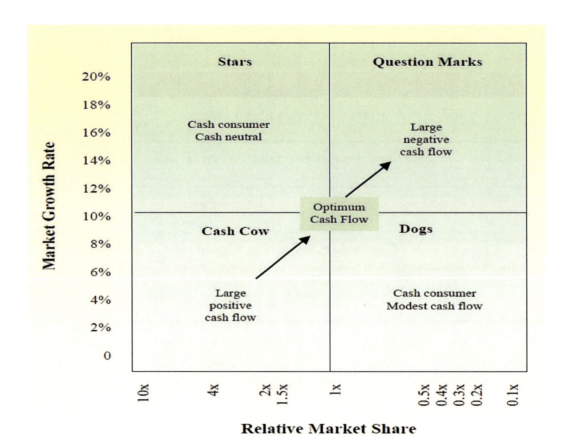

Figure 17: Boston Consulting Group Matrix

The BCG growth/share matrix is divided into four cells or quadrants, each of which represents a particular type of business:

Dogs: *Low Market Share / Low Market Growth*

In these areas, your market presence is weak, so it's going to take a lot of hard work to get noticed. You won't enjoy the scale economies of the larger players, so it's going to be difficult to make a profit. And because market growth is low, it's going to take a lot of hard work to improve the situation.

Cash Cows: *High Market Share / Low Market Growth*

Here, you're well-established, so it's easier to get attention and exploit new opportunities. However, it's only worth expending a certain amount of effort, because the market isn't growing, and your opportunities are limited.

Stars: *High Market Share / High Market Growth*

Here you're well-established, and growth is exciting! There should be some strong opportunities here, and you should work hard to realize them.

Question Marks (Problem Child): *Low Market Share / High Market Growth*

These are the opportunities no one knows what to do with. They aren't generating much revenue right now because you don't have a large market share. But, they are in high growth markets so the potential to make money is there.

Calculating McDonald's BCG Growth-Share Matrix

Market growth rate:

Relative market share:

Is found by dividing McDonald's Corporation market share, which is 12.9% by its closest competitor - Yum! Brands Inc. at 9.7%.

12.9/9.7 = 1.33

Based on the market growth rate, which is 2.0% and the relative market share of McDonald's Corporation of 1.33, McDonald's is located in the lower-left quadrant and is considered a cash cow.

McDonald's has a high relative market share in low growth fast food restaurants industry. As the market matures the need for investment reduces. The situation is frequently boosted by economies of scale that may be present with McDonald's which results to having restaurants in over 119 countries around the world and serving more than 64 million people per day.

Figure 18: Cash Cow Portrait

Determine what you will do with each product/product line. There are typically four different strategies to apply:

- **Build Market Share:** Make further investments (for example, to maintain Star status, or to turn a Question Mark into a Star).
- **Hold:** Maintain the status quo (do nothing).
- **Harvest:** Reduce the investment (enjoy positive cash flow and maximize profits from a Star or a Cash Cow).
- **Divest:** For example, get rid of the Dogs, and use the capital you receive to invest in Stars and Question Marks.

Rumelt's Criteria

Richard P. Rumelt is a professor at the Anderson School of Business at the University of California Los Angeles (UCLA). He developed four criteria to use in the evaluation of a business strategy: consistency, consonance, feasibility and advantage. The Rumelt method is used to evaluate a business strategy by assessing the strategy on each of these four criteria.

Consistency

Are the external strategies consistent with (supported by) the various internal aspects of the organization? You must examine all the various functional and internal management strategies employed by the organization and compare them with the external business strategy.

Consonance

Are the strategies in agreement with the various external trends (and sets of trends) in the environment? To answer these questions, you need to look at all the major trends that impact the selected strategy - both positively and negatively.

Feasibility

Is the strategy reasonable in terms of the organization's resources?

- Money and capital
- Management, professional, and technical resources
- Time span

Advantage

Does the strategy create and/or maintain a competitive advantage?

- Resources
- Skills
- Position

Figure 19: Innovation Cartoon

Rumelt's Criteria
McDonald's Corporation

Strategy	Consistency	Consonance	Feasibility	Advantage	Total
Market Penetrations					
Gaining competitors customers	5	4	5	4	18
Increasing Advertising	5	4	4	4	17
Market Development					
Global Expansion	5	5	5	4	19
Reaching into New Market Segments	4	3	3	4	14
Product Development					
Permanent Products (Big Mac, Quarter Pounder)	5	5	5	4	19
Temporary Products (McRib, Shamrock Shake)	4	4	3	3	14
Local Product Development (McKroket, McLobster)	4	4	4	4	16
Local Adaptation	5	4	5	5	19

As one can observe from the graph above, McDonald's has different business strategies in such areas as market penetrations, market development and product development. By assigning numbers 1-5 with 5 being the highest and 1 being the lowest, you will rate the importance of each strategy. After totaling the numbers you will get a good sense of which strategies to take action forward and which strategies to probably put on hold.

Strategies that scored the highest number of points include global expansion, permanent products and local adaptation. Such strategies are very important to McDonald's Corporation and its success in the future.

Competitive Position

Having a competitive advantage is necessary for a firm to compete in the market. But what is more important is whether the competitive advantage is sustainable. A company must identify its position relative to the competition in the market. By knowing if it is a leader, challenger, follower or nicher, it can adopt appropriate strategies to compete.

Genre of Market Position

Leader: Largest share

Challenger: Medium share, to challenge the leader

Follower: No offensive posture against the leader

Nicher: Small market size, segmentation other firms cannot think of

Relative Position Of Managerial Resources		Quantity	
		Large	Small
Quality	High	Leader	Nicher
	Low	Challenger	Follower

Figure 20: Matrix of Market Position/Managerial Resources

McDonald's is a market leader because:

- It has sustainable and superior sales. Over the past three years its sales have continued to grow and are much higher than its competitor's sales;
- It has the highest and leading market share with approximately 12.9% of the entire share in the fast food industry over its competitors.

Generic Competitive Strategies

The generic competitive strategies form a business tool which helps strategists understand how the position of a company within its industry can be directly related to the strategy it employs. The strategy employed can then be analyzed to understand where a company's competitive advantage lies, with a view to maintaining it. Porter (1985) identified the two main types of competitive advantage as cost advantage and differentiation. In developing and maintaining their competitive advantage, companies have the option to adopt one of the three generic strategies: cost leadership, differentiation or focus. The horizontal axis across the top of the graph shows the type of competitive advantage the company has, whilst the vertical axis relates to the scope of the competition, either broad and company-wide or narrow and limited to a market segment.

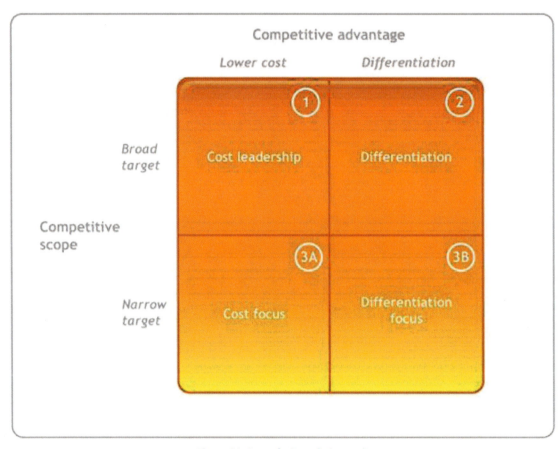

Figure 21: Porter's Generic Strategies

Cost Leadership

This is a strategy where a company aims to out-price its competitors by reducing overheads or the fixed costs associated with manufacture and distribution. It requires a focus on the efficiency of production lines and economies of scale. This strategy is employed where customers have the ability to change supplier easily and the products or services are standardized and well understood by the consumer. A good example of cost leadership strategy is employed by supermarket chains on everyday necessity goods. By using this strategy, marketing the product becomes less important. Benefits include raising barriers for competitors to enter the market and easing the effect of fixed-cost rises across the industry.

Differentiation

This strategy is employed where a unique attribute of a product or service is highlighted relative to similar alternatives presented by the competition. It allows a higher price to be charged or a greater ability to command customer loyalty. Differentiation strategy is used where the company sees its key product competencies as a more profitable advantage than simple cost leadership. Examples include Coca-Cola, which differentiates by building a solid brand, or Sony, which differentiates on quality or reliability of products. It relies heavily on marketing or advertising to maintain the brand identity and raises the barrier to competitors entering the market.

Focus

This strategy is aimed at a specific target consumer group, for example cultural, economic, political, geographical or age-related groups. The strategy employs either cost focus (3A) or differentiation focus (3B) within its target audience, and in this sense it is a narrower application of one of the aforementioned strategies.

McDonald's is a leader in using a differentiation strategy. McDonalds is differentiated by its very brand name and brand images of Big Mac and Ronald McDonald. McDonald's uses its vast and different menu items to differentiate itself against its competitors. For example, McDonald's launched oatmeal nationwide in 2011 as part of its differentiation strategy.

IV. Decisions and Recommendation

Best strategic alternatives for corporate, business, and functional.

Corporate

McDonald's Corporation uses a single business unit strategy. In an effort to make the traditional business model less bureaucratic and more flexible, McDonald's Corporation has begun implementing single business unit strategy. Instead of forcing a new department into the standard chain of command, the corporation will form differently sized autonomous business units that report directly to top management. Now the role of the corporation is to manage its business units and coordinate their efforts into the overall corporate strategy.

Business

For its business strategy, McDonald's will continue to implement its 'Plan to Win' strategy. The Plan to Win addresses the key drivers of McDonald's business and results—people, products, place, price and promotion. As part of this strategy, McDonald's will focus on quality, rather than overextension through uncontrollable growth.

Functional

McDonald's will continue to implement a functional strategy based on differentiation. A strong and well-known brand name as well as rich and unique menu items will help McDonald's continue such a strategy which will lead to higher market share in the fast food restaurants industry as well as higher sales, revenues and profits for the company as a whole. McDonald's functional strategies are all successfully co-aligned with their new generic strategy of marketing differentiation focusing on quality customer experiences.

Figure 22: McDonald's sandwiches

V. Implementation

Goals, Participants, Steps

Goal #1

Increase brand relevance and market share with operational and financial discipline through three global priorities: optimizing menu, modernizing the customer experience and broadening accessibility.

Participants

Everyone will have to be involved in the process in order for the strategy to be successful. Most of the changes will be implemented by higher management but in order for the changes to be sustainable, everyone in the company, including restaurant crew, will have to show support and commitment.

Steps

The menu efforts will include expanding destination beverages and desserts and enhancing the food image. The customer experience efforts will include accelerating the interior and exterior reimaging efforts and providing the restaurant teams with the appropriate tools, training, technology and staffing. The accessibility efforts will include increasing the level and variety of conveniences provided to the customers through greater proximity extended operating hours and stronger value platforms.

Figure 23: McDonald's restaurant in Tukwila, WA

Goal #2

Elevate the brand experience through information technology.

Participants

The new technology will be created by the R&D department and will be used daily by the restaurant staff from crew members to store managers and even possibly customers.

Steps

Leveraging the new point-of-sale system which allows the company to continue expanding its menu offerings while making it easier for the crew to fulfill every order accurately. Self-order kiosks and hand-held order devices will also be used to enhance the customer experience and help drive increased transactions and labor efficiency.

Goal #3

Produce biodiesel using recycled vegetable oil from McDonald's fast food restaurants located in the United Arab Emirates.

Participants

McDonald's UAE, a unit of Oak Brook, Illinois-based McDonald's Corporation, and Neutral Group, a Dubai parent company of Neutral Fuels that specializes in the optimization of energy and sustainability parameters for the global supply chain industry.

Steps

The joint venture was formed in July, 2011 between McDonald's UAE and Neutral Fuels LLC. The deal was worked discussed during several negotiation meetings between Karl Feilder, chairman of Neutral Group, and Rafic Fakih, Managing Director of McDonald's UAE.

VI. Works Cited

"DATAMONITOR: Mcdonald's Corporation." Mcdonald's Corporation SWOT Analysis (2011): 1-10. Business Source Complete. Web. 24 Apr. 2012.

"Disclosure SEC Database." LexisNexisÂ® Academic & Library Solutions. LexisNexisÂ® Academic & Library Solutions, 6 Sept. 2011. Web. 24 Apr. 2012. <http://www.lexisnexis.com/hottopics/lnacademic/>.

"LexisNexisÂ® Academic & Library Solutions." Worldscope. LexisNexisÂ® Academic & Library Solutions, 19 Mar. 2012. Web. 24 Apr. 2012. <http://www.lexisnexis.com/hottopics/lnacademic/>.

"Mcdonald's: A Global Brand At An Attractive Price." Black Book - U.S. Restaurants: Ordering From The Bernstein Value Menu (2010): 85-113. Business Source Complete. Web. 24 Apr. 2012.

"Mcdonald's Corporation." Mcdonald's Corporation SWOT Analysis (2008): 1-9. Business Source Complete. Web. 24 Apr. 2012.

"Home :: McDonalds.com." 302 Moved Temporarily. McDonald's Corporation, 2010-2012. Web. 24 Apr. 2012. <http://www.mcdonalds.com/us/en/home.html>.

Samadi, Nima. "Fast Food Restaurants in the US." IBISWorld Industry Report 72221a. IBISworld: Where Knowledge Is Power, Apr. 2012. Web. 24 Apr. 2012. <http://clients.ibisworld.com/industryus/default.aspx?indid=1980>.

TĂLPĂU, A., and D. BOŞCOR. "Customer-Oriented Marketing - A Strategy That Guarantees Success: Starbucks And Mcdonald's." Bulletin Of The Transilvania University Of Brasov. Series V: Economic Sciences 4.1 (2011): 51-58. Business Source Complete. Web. 24 Apr. 2012.

Made in the USA
Coppell, TX
11 May 2024

32275086R00048